UNDER HIS WINGS

A Synopsis of Emily Compagno's Inspiring Tribute to the Enduring Role of Faith in Military Life

AUSTIN C. BROOKS

Table Of Contents

INTRODUCTION

Faith and Freedom

Faith has been a cornerstone of the American military experience, offering strength, hope, and resilience to soldiers navigating the uncertainties of war. In Under His Wings: How Faith on the Front Lines Has Protected American Troops, Emily Compagno explores this profound connection, reflecting on her family's military heritage and her personal encounters with troops overseas.

Drawing on generations of stories, the introduction sets the tone for a book that blends historical and personal narratives. It highlights how faith has been a guiding light for soldiers, offering solace during times of separation, courage in the face of danger, and unity among comrades. The chapter underscores the enduring bond between spirituality and service, serving as a tribute to the sacrifices and spirit of America's heroes.

Overview of the role of faith in the U.S. military.

Faith has long been a vital source of strength and resilience for members of the U.S. military. From the trenches of World War I to modern-day conflicts, belief in a higher power has provided soldiers with hope and purpose during times of extreme hardship. Faith serves multiple roles:

1. **Emotional Resilience:** During combat, many soldiers turn to prayer, scripture, or chaplains for comfort and courage in the face of fear and loss. Spiritual practices help them process the emotional toll of war and stay grounded in difficult circumstances.

2. **Community and Unity:** Shared faith fosters camaraderie among troops. Chaplains, religious services, and prayer gatherings create opportunities for soldiers to support one another, forming bonds that transcend individual beliefs.

3. **Motivation and Sacrifice:** For many, faith is a guiding principle that inspires a sense of duty and willingness to serve. Belief in a divine purpose often strengthens their resolve to protect others, even at great personal cost.

4. **Family Connection:** Spirituality bridges the gap between soldiers and their families, as shared prayers and religious rituals offer comfort during long separations.

Faith is not merely a private solace but a collective force that unites troops and helps them endure the realities of service. Emily Compagno's Under His Wings explores this enduring role, showcasing the profound impact of spirituality on the lives of American service members across generations.

Personal Connections and Motivations of the Author

Emily Compagno's connection to the stories in Under His Wings is deeply personal. She comes from a family with a strong military heritage, with ancestors who served in both the Navy and Army. This legacy instilled in her a profound respect for the sacrifices and resilience of servicemembers.

Compagno's motivation for writing the book also stems from her own experiences visiting troops overseas. During her time as an Oakland Raiders cheerleader, she toured Iraq and Kuwait, witnessing firsthand the challenges faced by soldiers in active combat zones. These visits left a lasting impression on her, particularly the ways faith helped soldiers maintain their strength, unity, and resolve.

Her work reflects a desire to honor the courage and spirituality of these men and women, highlighting the enduring role of faith in their lives. By sharing their stories, she aims to celebrate their sacrifices while inspiring readers with tales of hope, camaraderie, and perseverance in the face of adversity.

Chapter 1: World War I

The Dawn of Battlefield Faith

World War I marked the beginning of large-scale modern warfare, exposing soldiers to unprecedented levels of danger and psychological strain. In this brutal environment, faith became an essential source of strength and solace for many service members.

1. Chaplains and Spiritual Guidance: Military chaplains played a critical role, providing spiritual support through prayer services, Bible studies, and one-on-one counseling. They often served alongside troops in the trenches, offering hope amidst chaos.

2. Letters and Religious Practices: Soldiers frequently wrote about their faith in letters home, describing how prayer and scripture helped them endure the horrors of war. Many carried pocket-sized Bibles or other religious tokens as constant reminders of their beliefs.

3. Faith as Resilience: The uncertainty of survival made faith a lifeline for soldiers facing death daily. Belief in a higher power gave them courage and a sense of purpose, helping them find meaning in their sacrifices.

The stories of faith during World War I, as highlighted in Emily Compagno's Under His Wings, show how spirituality offered soldiers a sense of stability and hope, even in the face of unimaginable adversity.

Stories of Soldiers Drawing Strength from Religious Beliefs during WWI.

During World War I, the relentless challenges of trench warfare, separation from loved ones, and the constant presence of death drove many soldiers to lean on their faith for strength and endurance. A few notable examples include:

1. The Christmas Truce of 1914: In one of the most famous moments of the war, opposing sides paused hostilities on Christmas Eve to share carols, prayers, and a temporary peace. This spontaneous act reflected a shared faith that transcended conflict and highlighted the human connection amidst war.

2. Personal Testimonies of Faith: Soldiers often wrote home about their reliance on prayer and scripture. One British soldier recounted how reading Psalms brought him comfort during bombings, while others described chaplain-led services as moments of solace and community in the trenches.

3. Carrying Religious Symbols: Many soldiers carried crosses, medals, or pocket Bibles into battle as tangible reminders of their beliefs.

These items provided a sense of protection and hope, grounding them during terrifying experiences.

4. Support from Chaplains: Military chaplains not only offered religious services but also tended to the emotional and spiritual needs of the troops. Stories emerged of chaplains praying with soldiers before battle or providing last rites, emphasizing their critical role in sustaining morale.

These accounts, highlighted in books like Emily Compagno's Under His Wings, reveal how faith helped soldiers navigate the physical and emotional toll of WWI, offering them courage and a sense of purpose amidst the chaos.

Chapter 2: World War II

Prayers in the Trenches

World War II, a global conflict of unprecedented scale, placed soldiers in physically and emotionally grueling situations. For many service members, prayer and faith became vital lifelines, providing the strength to persevere and face the horrors of war.

1. Faith in the Face of Danger: Stories from the frontlines recount soldiers praying together before missions or seeking solace through individual reflection. In letters home, troops often described how their faith brought comfort and courage during battles, such as the D-Day landings or the brutal Pacific campaigns.

2. Chaplains as Beacons of Hope: Military chaplains were indispensable in providing spiritual guidance. They held services in bombed-out churches, on warships, and even on the battlefield. Chaplains offered prayers, conducted funerals, and provided words of encouragement, reminding soldiers of the higher purpose behind their sacrifices.

3. Famous Accounts of Prayer: Leaders like General Dwight D. Eisenhower acknowledged the importance of faith, with Eisenhower famously calling for prayer on the eve of D-Day. Stories of entire platoons praying before critical missions underscore the widespread reliance on spirituality among the troops.

4. Religious Symbols as Guardians: Many soldiers carried religious items, such as crosses or pocket-sized Bibles, which served as sources of protection and comfort. For some, these symbols became cherished keepsakes that reminded them of their loved ones and beliefs.

Through its focus on firsthand accounts and historical moments, Emily Compagno's Under His Wings illustrates how faith sustained soldiers during the most harrowing moments of WWII, reaffirming its critical role in military life.

Accounts of Servicemen Relying on Faith Amidst Global Conflict

The global scale and relentless brutality of World War II drove many servicemen to rely on their faith as a source of strength, courage, and hope. Personal accounts reveal how spirituality provided emotional resilience during some of history's darkest times:

1. Prayers on the Battlefield: Soldiers often turned to prayer before engaging in dangerous missions. On the beaches of Normandy during D-Day, many servicemen knelt in silent prayer, seeking divine guidance and protection in the face of overwhelming odds.

2. Letters Reflecting Faith: Written correspondence between soldiers and their families frequently highlighted their reliance on spiritual beliefs. One soldier, stationed in Europe, wrote to his family about how reciting the 23rd Psalm calmed his nerves before combat.

3. Chaplains Providing Spiritual Support: Chaplains played pivotal roles in maintaining soldiers' morale, leading services in makeshift chapels or directly on the frontlines. For example, Chaplain George L. Fox, one of the "Four Chaplains" aboard the USAT Dorchester, sacrificed his life by giving up his life jacket while praying alongside fellow servicemen during a shipwreck.

4. Faith in Captivity: Prisoners of war often clung to their beliefs as a source of hope. In Japanese and German POW camps, servicemen secretly held prayer gatherings and shared scripture, finding unity and strength in their faith despite the harsh conditions.

5. Religious Artifacts as Symbols of Hope: Many soldiers carried pocket-sized Bibles, rosaries, or crosses, using these items as tangible reminders of their faith and loved ones. These small tokens were cherished as sources of comfort in the chaos of war.

These stories, highlighted in works like Emily Compagno's Under His Wings, illustrate how faith became an anchor for soldiers amidst the uncertainty and devastation of World War II, sustaining them through moments of fear and sacrifice.

Chapter 3: Korea and Vietnam

Faith Through the Fire

The Korean and Vietnam Wars introduced soldiers to new forms of warfare, hostile terrains, and grueling conditions, testing their resilience like never before. Amid the turmoil, many servicemen turned to faith as a source of strength, solace, and guidance.

1. Faith in the Face of Isolation: Both wars were marked by extreme isolation, with soldiers often feeling detached from their homes and the world. In letters home, many servicemen described how prayer and scripture sustained them during long nights and in moments of doubt.

2. Chaplains in Action: Military chaplains remained a crucial presence, conducting religious services in combat zones, providing emotional support, and offering spiritual guidance. In Korea, chaplains like Emil Kapaun gained legendary status for their bravery and unwavering dedication to soldiers' spiritual and physical well-being.

3. Prayer in Crisis: Soldiers in Vietnam often relied on prayer during ambushes and guerrilla attacks. Stories emerged of small groups praying together in foxholes or reciting Psalms to maintain calm under fire.

4. Faith as a Unifying Force: In the face of cultural and political divisions back home, faith provided a unifying thread among soldiers. Religious practices created a shared space for reflection, offering troops a sense of community in the hostile environments of Korea and Vietnam.

5. Religious Tokens of Protection: Soldiers frequently carried religious items such as crucifixes, medals, and Bibles as symbols of hope and protection. These artifacts became deeply personal reminders of their beliefs and the loved ones praying for their safe return.

Emily Compagno's Under His Wings highlights how faith remained a steadfast source of strength during these wars, helping servicemen endure physical and emotional challenges while fostering resilience and camaraderie.

How Belief in God Offered Solace in Tumultuous Wars

In the challenging environments of the Korean and Vietnam Wars, where soldiers faced harsh climates, unpredictable guerrilla warfare, and psychological strain, belief in God provided comfort and strength. Many servicemen leaned on their faith to navigate the fear and uncertainty of these conflicts.

1. A Source of Comfort: For soldiers stationed far from home, belief in God offered a sense of stability. Whether through personal prayer or communal worship, faith reminded them they were not alone, even in the most isolating circumstances.

2. Chaplains as Spiritual Anchors: Military chaplains in both wars worked tirelessly to support troops, often conducting services in combat zones. They offered soldiers opportunities to pray, confess, and discuss their fears, creating an emotional refuge amidst chaos.

3. Faith During Combat: Soldiers often turned to prayer during moments of danger. Many recounted how belief in divine protection gave them the courage to face intense battles and the strength to keep moving forward.

4. Hope in Captivity: Prisoners of war, particularly in Vietnam, found solace in faith during their captivity. Shared prayers, hymns, and scripture passages provided hope and a means of emotional survival under brutal conditions.

5. Connection to Home: Faith also served as a link to loved ones. Letters from home frequently mentioned prayers for safety, which became sources of reassurance for soldiers. Their own prayers often centered on their families, creating a sense of spiritual connection across the distance.

These personal and collective acts of faith underscored the role of spirituality in sustaining soldiers through the physical and emotional toll of these tumultuous wars. Emily Compagno's Under His Wings captures the enduring power of belief in God to provide solace and strength during such defining conflicts.

Chapter 4: Modern Wars

Iraq and Afghanistan

The wars in Iraq and Afghanistan introduced soldiers to unique challenges, including insurgencies, prolonged deployments, and the mental strain of asymmetrical warfare. Despite these difficulties, faith played a critical role in helping servicemembers navigate the physical and emotional toll of combat.

1. Faith as Resilience in Combat: Many soldiers deployed to Iraq and Afghanistan reported relying on prayer and scripture to stay grounded amidst the uncertainty of daily missions. The ever-present threat of IEDs, ambushes, and extended tours often drew troops closer to their beliefs.

2. Support from Chaplains: Chaplains continued their pivotal role in these modern conflicts, holding religious services on forward operating bases (FOBs) and accompanying troops on dangerous patrols. Their presence provided spiritual support and moments of peace amidst the chaos.

3. Shared Spiritual Practices: Group prayers before missions and in the aftermath of attacks helped foster unity among soldiers. Such practices reminded troops of their shared humanity and provided a sense of purpose beyond the immediate conflict.

4. Coping with Trauma: Faith became a vital coping mechanism for soldiers dealing with PTSD and the emotional scars of war. Many turned to God for healing, seeking solace in religious practices or through chaplain counseling sessions.

5. Faith on the Home Front: Families of deployed troops often found comfort in their own faith, praying for their loved ones' safety and leaning on spiritual communities for support. Soldiers cherished these connections, drawing strength from the knowledge that prayers were being offered on their behalf.

Emily Compagno's Under His Wings highlights the personal stories of service members who found strength through their belief in God during these modern wars, showcasing the continued importance of faith in sustaining the military's spirit and resolve.

Personal Anecdotes from Troops in Modern Conflicts

In the wars in Iraq and Afghanistan, many service members shared deeply personal stories of how faith helped them cope with the unique challenges of modern warfare. These anecdotes highlight the emotional and spiritual resilience soldiers relied on during combat.

1. Prayers for Protection: One soldier stationed in Iraq recalled the moments before a mission, when he and his squad gathered in a circle to pray for protection. The constant threat of roadside bombs and sniper fire made these prayers a source of peace, giving the men courage to face the uncertainty of each day.

2. A Soldier's Conversion: Another poignant story comes from a soldier who, during his deployment in Afghanistan, experienced a profound spiritual awakening. Initially skeptical of religion, he found himself attending chapel services regularly after witnessing the steadfast faith of fellow soldiers. The chaplain's words during a particularly difficult period of conflict helped him find a new sense of purpose and connection to God.

3. Strength Amidst Grief: A medic shared how he relied on his Christian faith during the traumatic experience of treating wounded soldiers. He often turned to prayer to help him cope with the overwhelming emotions of loss and fear, finding comfort in the belief that his actions were part of a larger divine plan.

4. Faith in Recovery: One soldier, struggling with PTSD after returning home, found solace in his faith, which he said became the anchor that kept him grounded through therapy and difficult emotional healing. His belief in God played a key role in his journey toward recovery, offering him hope for the future.

These stories, as featured in works like Under His Wings, illustrate how soldiers' faith in God provided not just physical protection, but emotional fortitude during their deployments, helping them cope with trauma and persevere through the hardships of modern combat.

Emily's Own Experiences with U.S. Soldiers as an NFL Cheerleader

Emily Compagno's connection to U.S. servicemembers deepened through her time as an NFL cheerleader, where she participated in USO tours to visit troops overseas. During her visits to Iraq and Kuwait, she witnessed firsthand the challenges soldiers faced and the role that faith played in their lives during deployment.

Through these experiences, Emily observed the spiritual strength and resilience of the troops, many of whom shared personal stories of how their belief in God kept them going through dangerous and isolating circumstances. These interactions deeply impacted her, inspiring her to write Under His Wings. The book highlights not only the soldiers' faith but also their camaraderie, resilience, and the profound sense of purpose they found in their military service, even in the most trying environments.

Compagno's time with the U.S. military in these settings cemented her admiration for the role faith plays in helping soldiers endure the hardships of war. Her personal connection to the troops adds an emotional depth to the book, as she integrates their stories of faith with her own experiences and reflections. These moments shaped her understanding of how spiritual beliefs offer strength on the front lines, influencing the tone and messages of her writing.

Chapter 5: Faith in Everyday Military Life

Faith plays a pivotal role in the everyday lives of servicemembers, providing them with resilience, purpose, and emotional support amidst the challenges of military life. From daily routines to long deployments, belief in God or a higher power serves as a source of strength for many in uniform.

1. Routine Spiritual Practices: Many soldiers incorporate faith into their daily lives, whether through morning prayers, reading scripture, or attending religious services. These rituals offer moments of peace and grounding amid the chaos of military life.

2. Chaplains' Role in the Military: Military chaplains are key figures in supporting the spiritual needs of soldiers, offering counseling, leading services, and providing a comforting presence. Chaplains are often seen as lifelines, helping troops cope with stress, loss, and uncertainty during deployments.

3. Faith as a Source of Unity: Shared religious practices, like group prayers before missions, foster camaraderie and a sense of purpose among soldiers. These moments of collective faith help build solidarity, providing emotional support and reinforcing the bonds between comrades.

4. Faith in Adversity: Soldiers often rely on their faith during particularly difficult or dangerous times. In moments of fear or loss, prayer and spiritual belief offer solace, whether it's to cope with the trauma of battle or to stay hopeful during long periods of separation from family.

Emily Compagno's Under His Wings sheds light on how faith provides crucial emotional and spiritual support, helping soldiers navigate the challenges of military life and survive the physical and psychological tolls of war. These everyday acts of faith illustrate the deep connection between belief and the resilience of those serving in the armed forces.

Letters, Chaplains' Roles, and Religious Practices on Deployment

During military deployments, soldiers rely heavily on spiritual support to navigate the difficulties they face. Letters from home, the presence of chaplains, and daily religious practices all play crucial roles in sustaining soldiers' faith and mental well-being.

1. Letters from Home: For many soldiers, letters from loved ones serve as a powerful reminder of home and the support they have waiting for them. These letters often contain prayers, religious encouragement, and words of comfort that reinforce their faith. Soldiers describe how receiving these letters—sometimes with scripture verses or messages of hope—helped them endure the isolation and hardships of deployment. These written connections are not just emotional lifelines, but spiritual support that bolsters their belief in a higher purpose during times of uncertainty and danger.

2. Chaplains' Roles: Military chaplains provide spiritual care by offering religious services, one-on-one counseling, and support for soldiers facing personal or moral crises. They serve as confidants and counselors, helping troops process grief, loss, and trauma. Chaplains also conduct religious services, especially in combat zones, and offer prayers for safety before missions. Their presence offers comfort, reassurance, and a safe space for soldiers to explore their faith. The emotional impact of chaplains' work is profound, as they help soldiers reconnect with their beliefs during times of stress.

3. Religious Practices on Deployment: Despite the challenges of being away from home, soldiers continue to practice their faith. Many participate in group prayers before missions, attend services held by chaplains, or find moments of solitude for personal reflection and prayer. Some carry religious symbols such as crosses or small Bibles, which provide comfort and a tangible connection to their beliefs. These practices help soldiers maintain a sense of normalcy, create a sense of unity, and provide mental resilience against the harsh conditions of war.

These elements of military life help soldiers endure the challenges of deployment. Emily Compagno's Under His Wings highlights the importance of faith in sustaining soldiers during these difficult times, showcasing the critical role of chaplains, letters, and religious practices in fostering hope, unity, and resilience.

Chapter 6: Celebrity Visits and Spiritual Upliftment

Celebrity visits to military personnel have long played an important role in boosting morale and offering spiritual upliftment to troops in combat zones. These visits, often organized through the USO (United Service Organizations), serve as a source of emotional and psychological support for service members far from home, providing moments of joy and a reminder of the appreciation and respect they have from the public.

1. Boosting Morale Through Connection: Celebrities, particularly those with ties to the entertainment industry, make it a priority to visit active-duty troops during their deployments. The presence of well-known figures provides soldiers with an emotional connection to the home front, reminding them that they are valued and appreciated. These visits also offer soldiers a brief escape from the harsh realities of combat, making them feel celebrated and supported.

2. Spiritual Upliftment: Many celebrities involved in these tours offer more than just entertainment; they bring a message of hope and inspiration. For example, religious figures or celebrities with strong spiritual beliefs often share messages of faith, deliver speeches, or lead brief prayer services. Some visits may include chaplain-led sessions, where celebrities participate, allowing soldiers to engage in worship, prayer, and reflection.

3. Personal Stories and Shared Faith: Celebrities who have experienced their own struggles with faith or adversity often relate their personal stories to soldiers. By sharing how faith has helped them through difficult times, they create a connection that transcends the celebrity-soldier divide, offering troops both a spiritual and emotional bond. These moments provide soldiers with a sense of comfort and encouragement, reinforcing the power of belief in times of trial.

4. Notable Visits and Impact: High-profile celebrity visits, such as those by Bob Hope during WWII or by more recent entertainers like Drew Carey and Jon Stewart in Iraq and Afghanistan, have been well-documented. These visits not only provide spiritual support but also help soldiers feel connected to a broader community of people who care about their well-being.

In Under His Wings, Emily Compagno also highlights the impact of these visits, sharing stories of how faith-based events led by celebrities and chaplains helped provide spiritual guidance and emotional healing for soldiers in active combat zones.

Stories of USO Tours Featuring Figures Like Marilyn Monroe and Ronald Reagan

The USO (United Service Organizations) has long been a source of comfort and morale-boosting for American soldiers, with celebrities offering their time and support through entertaining performances, visits, and acts of kindness. Figures like Marilyn Monroe and Ronald Reagan played key roles in these tours, providing emotional upliftment and spiritual encouragement to troops during wartime.

1. Marilyn Monroe's Visit to Korea: One of the most iconic USO moments occurred when Marilyn Monroe visited U.S. troops in Korea in 1954. As part of her tour, Monroe performed for thousands of servicemen, bringing glamour, joy, and a sense of normalcy to those stationed in a war zone. Her performances were not only entertaining but also deeply symbolic of the connection between home and the frontlines, offering soldiers a brief respite from the hardship of the Korean War. Monroe's warmth, charm, and attention to the troops made her a beloved figure in military circles, and her visit is still remembered as one of the most uplifting moments for U.S. forces during the 1950s.

2. Ronald Reagan's USO Involvement: Before becoming president, Ronald Reagan was actively involved in the USO, participating in multiple tours to entertain and support soldiers. In the 1940s, as a young actor and former Army Reservist, Reagan toured military bases, visiting servicemen both stateside and overseas. His visits during World War II helped boost troop morale, and his ability to connect with soldiers on a personal level made him a popular figure. Reagan's speeches and camaraderie with the troops offered them not only a sense of patriotism and gratitude but also spiritual encouragement, as he frequently spoke of the values that the U.S. military stood for.

3. The Legacy of USO Celebrities: Monroe and Reagan's tours, along with others, demonstrate how entertainment and faith-based encouragement went hand in hand. USO tours not only provided a distraction from the hardships of war but also reinforced the importance of faith, hope, and patriotism in the lives of soldiers. These visits, while often light-hearted in nature, carried deeper emotional significance, allowing troops to feel connected to their home country and the people they were fighting for.

These stories exemplify the important role that celebrity involvement in the USO plays in uplifting the spirits of soldiers during their deployments. Both Monroe and Reagan remain symbols of how entertainment and spiritual support can be a powerful force in wartime morale.

Chapter 7: The Enduring Spirit of Camaraderie and Sacrifice

The enduring spirit of camaraderie and sacrifice is a core aspect of military life, especially during times of war. Throughout history, soldiers have formed deep, unbreakable bonds that transcend the hardships they face, and their willingness to sacrifice for each other and for a greater cause is a testament to the strength of human connection in extreme circumstances.

1. Shared Experiences and Brotherhood: In every major conflict, from World War I to the modern-day wars in Iraq and Afghanistan, the shared experiences of soldiers foster a unique bond. Soldiers rely on one another for emotional support, and the camaraderie they form on the battlefield often becomes the strongest foundation for their survival. These connections are often strengthened by common beliefs, including faith, as soldiers support each other through spiritual practices like prayer or religious services.

2. Sacrifice for the Greater Good: Military sacrifice is often viewed through the lens of duty and loyalty. Soldiers consistently put themselves in harm's way to protect their comrades, the mission, and their country. This sense of selflessness is a recurring theme, often reinforced by spiritual beliefs that inspire soldiers to endure and push forward even in the face of danger. Faith and sacrifice go hand in hand, as many soldiers find strength in the belief that their actions have a higher purpose.

3. Stories of Sacrifice and Solidarity: From the trenches of World War I to the deserts of Iraq, countless stories highlight the personal sacrifices made by soldiers for each other. Chaplains, often seen as both spiritual guides and confidants, play a pivotal role in this sense of solidarity. They not only provide religious services but also serve as witnesses to the sacrifices soldiers make, often staying with them during some of the most perilous moments.

In Under His Wings, Emily Compagno highlights how faith, coupled with a strong sense of camaraderie, has been a source of resilience for soldiers across generations. Their shared belief systems and willingness to make the ultimate sacrifice for their comrades create a legacy of courage, selflessness, and spiritual fortitude in military history.

Accounts of Shared Faith Fostering Unity Among Troops

Faith has played a significant role in fostering unity among troops across various conflicts. Shared religious beliefs and practices often serve as powerful bonding agents, strengthening soldiers' camaraderie and providing emotional and spiritual support during times of hardship.

1. World War I – Faith in the Trenches: During World War I, soldiers in the trenches often turned to faith as a way to cope with the intense stress and danger surrounding them. Many units held group prayers before going into battle, finding strength in the shared act of worship. Accounts from soldiers reveal how religious services in the trenches not only provided spiritual solace but also reinforced a sense of brotherhood. A shared belief in divine protection and a common goal of survival brought soldiers together, transcending individual fears and offering them the courage to face the horrors of war.

2. World War II – Unity Through Shared Belief: In World War II, faith again served as a unifying force for troops. As soldiers faced overwhelming odds, they often turned to prayer to maintain hope and resilience. Chaplains played a critical role in facilitating these acts of worship, organizing services that brought soldiers together and offered both spiritual and emotional support. Many soldiers recall praying together before dangerous missions, drawing strength from the collective faith of their comrades. This shared spirituality fostered a deep sense of unity, helping soldiers confront the challenges of global conflict.

3. The Vietnam War – Faith in the Face of Trauma: In the Vietnam War, where the psychological and emotional toll on soldiers was particularly severe, faith-based unity remained essential. Many soldiers, experiencing the trauma of guerrilla warfare and unpredictable violence, found comfort in religious practices and shared spiritual experiences. Chaplains provided vital support, offering counseling and conducting worship services. Soldiers recount how, in the midst of violence, prayer sessions helped to soothe their fears, making them feel united in their faith and stronger together. These shared moments of worship created a sense of solidarity among soldiers, even as they dealt with the moral and physical challenges of the war.

4. Modern Wars – Iraq and Afghanistan: In recent conflicts in Iraq and Afghanistan, shared faith has continued to be a powerful force. Soldiers report relying on group prayers and Bible studies to help them endure long deployments and dangerous missions. The presence of chaplains in the field has remained a crucial element in offering both spiritual and emotional support. Troops often find themselves united by their faith during times of hardship, whether through shared prayer before missions or during quiet moments of reflection. The act of coming together to pray offers soldiers a sense of peace and strengthens their bonds of trust, reinforcing their collective resolve to protect each other and their mission.

5. Wartime Hymns and Songs: Music played a significant role in fostering unity among troops during wartime, particularly through hymns and religious songs. Soldiers often sang together in the trenches, choosing hymns like "Abide with Me" and "Onward, Christian Soldiers" that reflected their shared faith and reinforced a collective sense of purpose. These songs provided comfort and a temporary escape from the grim realities of war, creating a momentary bond that transcended individual fears.

In some instances, hymns were sung during impromptu memorial services for fallen comrades, where soldiers of diverse backgrounds joined voices in mourning and hope. Singing together not only helped soldiers process grief but also reinforced their belief in a higher purpose, offering a profound sense of spiritual connection and unity in the face of shared adversity.

This act of collective worship through song became an enduring symbol of the resilience and solidarity nurtured by shared faith. It reminded soldiers that even in the darkest times, their bond with one another and their connection to their spiritual beliefs could sustain them.

In Emily Compagno's Under His Wings, many of these personal accounts are shared, emphasizing the role of faith in bringing troops together and sustaining them through the most trying times of their service. The strength derived from shared belief has been vital in maintaining unity among soldiers, allowing them to endure the hardships of war with a sense of purpose and spiritual support.

Chapter 8: Family and Homefront

The Role of Faith in Separation

Faith serves as a vital support system for both soldiers and their families during times of separation, particularly in the context of long deployments. While soldiers face the challenges of combat, their families also navigate emotional and spiritual struggles on the homefront. The role of faith helps both groups cope with the hardships that come with being apart.

1. Strength for Families: For families left behind, faith becomes a foundation of hope and resilience. Many spouses, children, and parents lean on their religious beliefs, praying for the safety and well-being of their loved ones deployed overseas. Faith provides them with comfort during times of uncertainty, as they find solace in the belief that their loved ones are being protected by divine guidance. Families often participate in church communities where they receive emotional and spiritual support, further reinforcing their faith during difficult times.

2. Spiritual Connection During Separation:

For service members, faith can bridge the emotional distance between them and their families. While on deployment, soldiers often turn to prayer and religious rituals to stay connected to their loved ones, even when separated by vast distances. Some soldiers write letters that include prayers or scripture verses, strengthening the spiritual bond between themselves and their families. The shared act of prayer—whether conducted via letters or phone calls—offers a sense of closeness and provides emotional support despite the separation.

3. Faith in Overcoming Loneliness and Fear:

Separation can create feelings of loneliness, fear, and isolation for both soldiers and their families. Soldiers, especially in combat zones, often rely on their faith to cope with the anxiety and stress of their environments. Prayer, meditation, and religious services conducted by chaplains provide soldiers with emotional solace and a sense of divine presence, helping them manage the psychological toll of deployment. For families, prayer becomes a way to stay spiritually connected to their loved ones, while simultaneously providing them with the strength to face their own challenges at home.

4. The Power of Church Communities: Many families find solace in their church communities, where they gather for support, prayer, and fellowship. These communities often organize prayer chains, send care packages, and offer counseling for families experiencing emotional distress. The support of a faith-based community creates a sense of shared purpose and strengthens the belief that they are not alone during the deployment.

In Under His Wings, Emily Compagno delves into how faith sustains both soldiers and their families, helping them cope with the challenges of separation and the emotional weight of war. The shared belief system between soldiers and their families not only provides comfort but also strengthens the emotional bonds that are essential to surviving the hardships of military life.

Letters and Stories Reflecting the Faith of Soldiers and Their Families

Letters exchanged between soldiers and their families during times of separation often contain deeply personal expressions of faith, offering comfort, encouragement, and hope in the face of adversity. These letters not only serve as emotional lifelines but also highlight the role of faith in maintaining strength and resilience during deployments.

1. Soldiers' Letters of Faith: Many soldiers write home about their reliance on prayer and spiritual beliefs during difficult moments in combat. For example, soldiers have written about their daily prayers for safety, asking for divine protection in the midst of dangerous operations. Some even send religious verses or passages to their families, reinforcing their connection to both their faith and loved ones. One soldier, writing from Iraq, expressed gratitude for the chaplain's services and shared how group prayers with fellow soldiers helped him maintain hope. These letters often speak of the solace soldiers found in their faith, especially when facing moments of intense fear or uncertainty.

2. Faith in Letters from Home: Letters from families also reflect the importance of faith during separation. Wives, parents, and children often express their prayers for their soldiers' safety, sharing verses from scripture or personal prayers. One letter from a wife to her husband serving overseas included a passage from Psalms, encouraging him to find peace in God's protection. These letters became cherished tokens of emotional support and spiritual connection, offering a sense of comfort that transcended the physical distance.

3. Stories of Soldiers' Faith: Many stories of soldiers in active duty highlight how faith helped them navigate the harsh realities of war. In the Vietnam War, for example, soldiers spoke of the impact of carrying a Bible or other religious items, using them as reminders of home and their shared belief system. One soldier recalled how he and his comrades would gather for impromptu prayer sessions in the jungle, finding strength in their shared faith as they faced danger together. These shared moments of prayer created bonds between soldiers, reminding them of their purpose and providing mental and emotional strength.

4. Faith as a Family Bond: For families, faith becomes a source of stability during prolonged separation. Parents often share stories of holding prayer vigils for their sons or daughters, hoping for their safe return. One mother, in a letter to her deployed son, spoke of the peace she found in knowing that her prayers were guiding him even in the midst of conflict. For many families, the shared practice of faith, whether through prayer chains or attending religious services, helped them cope with the uncertainty of having a loved one in a dangerous environment.

In Under His Wings, Emily Compagno explores these personal stories of faith, highlighting how letters and shared prayers sustain both soldiers and their families during deployments. These letters serve not only as a connection to loved ones but also as a reminder of the power of faith to bring comfort, hope, and strength in the most challenging of circumstances.

Conclusion

The Power of Prayer and Gratitude

The enduring power of prayer and gratitude is a central theme throughout Under His Wings by Emily Compagno. Both faith and thankfulness serve as critical tools for soldiers and their families, providing the emotional and spiritual fortitude to endure the challenges of military life and warfare. Prayer offers soldiers a source of strength during times of fear and uncertainty, while gratitude helps them remain grounded in the midst of hardship.

1. The Power of Prayer: Prayer has been a consistent source of comfort and guidance for military personnel, offering them a moment of peace and connection with something greater than themselves. Whether through private moments of reflection or shared group prayers, soldiers turn to prayer to cope with the stress of combat and separation from loved ones. Through these spiritual practices, they are able to find strength, courage, and resilience. Chaplains, too, play an essential role in facilitating prayer and spiritual care, further reinforcing the power of faith in maintaining morale and mental health.

2. Gratitude in the Face of Adversity: In addition to prayer, gratitude remains a key aspect of soldiers' spiritual lives. Many troops express thanks for the opportunity to serve their country, for the protection they receive, and for the support of their families and faith communities. These expressions of gratitude, even during times of hardship, foster a sense of purpose and help soldiers remain focused on the greater mission. Gratitude also strengthens the bonds between soldiers, as they share moments of thanks together, reinforcing the collective resilience they have in facing adversity.

3. The Emotional and Spiritual Impact: Both prayer and gratitude offer profound emotional and spiritual relief. These practices provide soldiers and their families with a sense of connection, whether through the act of praying together or through the quiet moments of thanksgiving. The emotional resilience cultivated through prayer and gratitude helps them navigate the immense challenges of war, while also strengthening their unity and sense of purpose.

In the stories shared throughout Under His Wings, Compagno highlights how these simple yet profound acts of faith—prayer and gratitude—have sustained soldiers throughout history. By turning to prayer and expressing gratitude for their blessings, troops find a source of strength and a reminder of the higher purpose they serve, ensuring that their spirits remain strong even in the darkest moments of conflict.

Reflections on the Enduring Legacy of Faith in Military Life

Faith has consistently played a vital role in the lives of military personnel, providing them with the strength, hope, and resilience needed to endure the challenges of warfare and separation from loved ones. The enduring legacy of faith in military life can be seen across generations, from World War I to modern-day conflicts in Iraq and Afghanistan. Through prayer, religious rituals, and shared belief, soldiers have found solace in times of fear, loss, and uncertainty. This spiritual foundation has not only helped them survive the physical and emotional hardships of war but has also fostered a sense of unity and camaraderie among troops.

1. A Source of Strength: Faith has been a consistent source of emotional and psychological strength for soldiers, offering them comfort in moments of despair. Whether it is through individual prayers for protection or communal worship, soldiers turn to their spiritual beliefs to navigate the trauma and uncertainty of combat. Religious rituals, such as services led by chaplains, have provided soldiers with a sense of peace and grounding, reminding them of their higher purpose.

2. Camaraderie and Unity: Shared faith has created strong bonds among soldiers, uniting them in the face of adversity. From the trenches of World War I to the deserts of Iraq, soldiers have come together to pray, share their faith, and support one another. This spiritual unity has been essential in maintaining morale and emotional well-being during some of the most challenging and dangerous times.

3. Family and Homefront: Faith has also played an important role on the homefront, where families have turned to prayer and religious practices to cope with the separation from their loved ones. Letters, care packages, and shared prayers between soldiers and their families have strengthened the emotional ties that bridge the distance of deployment. For many families, faith has provided a sense of hope and connection, even when facing the uncertainty of war.

4. The Role of Chaplains: Chaplains have been an integral part of military life, offering both spiritual guidance and emotional support to soldiers. They provide religious services, counseling, and a listening ear during the toughest moments, ensuring that soldiers have access to the spiritual resources they need. Chaplains are a key part of maintaining the legacy of faith within military culture, often being the ones who organize prayer sessions, offer comfort, and remind soldiers of the greater purpose they serve.

In Under His Wings, Emily Compagno reflects on the profound impact that faith has had on military life, sharing personal stories and historical accounts that highlight the spiritual resilience of soldiers. This legacy of faith continues to shape the military experience, providing soldiers with the strength to face challenges, the hope to endure, and the community to support them through difficult times.

Made in the USA
Columbia, SC
15 December 2024

49318163R00030